Uncle Rob's Picture

Uncle Rob's Picture

Book 1 – Daley News Essays

F. Darnall Daley, Jr.

2021

Book Cover Designed
F. Darnall Daley, Jr.
F. D. Daley & Associates
Cover Photo – by F. Darnall Daley, Jr.
Anthony van Dyke – "Portrait of Mary Ruthven,
wife of the artist (Uncle Rob's picture)

ISBN: 9798737505813

Dedication

To my bride of over 63 years, Mary Ernestine "Ernie" Daley and to my friend Robert "Bob" Dorn whose idea of weekly emails I unashamedly stole.

Contents

Other books by F. Darnall Daley, Jr.

Non-Fiction:
- ❖ The Commissioner's Corner – A collection of inspirational essays (2007)
- ❖ MyEasyJobSearch.com – How to get a job in the 21st Century (2011)
  (With F. D. "Dale" Daley. III)
- ❖ Rules for Life – Including Darnall's Rules (2018)
- ❖ My Name Is Frank – Biography and Sermons of The Rev. Francis D. Daley (2020)
- ❖ Alcoholism – The Rev. Francis D. Daley's Sermons (2020)
- ❖ A Friend of Bill's – The Rev. Francis Darnall Daley (2020)
- ❖ Have you Ever Been Afraid – The Rev. Francis D. Daley's Sermons (2020)
- ❖ The Tooth of Time – A Collection of Poems (2020)

Journals:
- ❖ Daily Diabetic Glucose Journal (2018)

Fiction:
- ❖ The Adventures of Alizar – The Beginning (2017)
- ❖ Alizar and the Crisis – An Alizar Adventure (2017)

All of these are available on Amazon, Kindle, and signed copies on ebay.

Introduction

This volume contains essays that were published in weekly emails to friends and family. My thought in writing and sending these emails was that if you want people to communicate with you, you have to start the conversation. In my youth communication was handwritten letters but today it's email. During the recent pandemic of 2020, I thought that it would be a good idea to find a way to keep in touch with family and friends. Fortunately, the internet provides us with a really good way to accomplish that.

At the same time, I got an email from my old friend Bob Dorn. Bob sends an email every Sunday morning at 9:00 AM to all of his friends. He picked this time because he used to call his father every Sunday at that same time.

So, I stole that idea from him.[1] I also remembered that when I was in the military boarding school, if you wanted to get letters, you had to write letters.

I also knew that if I was going to write emails to friends and family, they had to be more than, "Hey, how are you?" So, I decided to write a series of essays that were at least mildly interesting. These I started out sending out every Tuesday. Later I

---

[1] Thanks, Bob.

began sending these out Tuesday and Friday. The subject line was "Daley News."

This volume is the first collection of those essays.

Pedicures[2]

Just a note to touch base and ask how you're doing.

Last week Ernie and I went for our his and her pedicures. For the last year or so we've been going together every 5 to 6 weeks. Part of our job in these visits is to entertain and regale the staff with tales of our teen years in boarding schools.   No colored polish for me, just for Ernie. Lately finding our favorite pedicurist, Nicol, has been an adventure. Two months ago, she texted us that she had moved to another salon. So, we made an appointment at that salon. That visit went off without a hitch. We made the next appointment.

At the appointed time for the second visit, we arrived to find the salon locked. When we rang the bell, the lady that answered told us that Nicol was no longer there. *Whisky Tango Foxtrot!* More text messages! She's at a different salon now. That's where we were this past week. Life is a grand adventure if you don't weaken.

---

2 Emailed to friends and family on March 10, 2020 - Daley News #1

Grocery Shopping[3]

In view of the coronavirus and the stock market dip, Ernie and I have had to make do with less help. Hence, we have been doing our own grocery shopping. And, boy, do we have a system! At home we make a written shopping list. Ernie carries the list and a pen to mark-off the items purchased.

As we hit the door, she gives me an assignment of 2 or 3 items. No more than that because as I explained she has the paper and pen, and memory is not what it used to be. Now there are some items that I haven't been trained on. For these she's on her own. For example, salad greens. These come in convenient bags. There are 27 different varieties. To me the names all seem the same. ("Butter Cup" "Butter Spring" "Spring Breeze") Another example, is paper plates. Did you know they come in different sizes? Sure, I know that NOW! Ernie knows not to give me assignments for which my training is inadequate. When I finish an assignment, I find her and get my next assignment.

In honor of Saint Patrick's Day, I close with - May the road rise up to meet you, May the wind be always at your back. May the sun shine warm upon your face, and the rains fall soft upon your fields.

---

[3] Emailed to friends and family on March 17, 2020 - Daley News #2

Books[4]

I was so disappointed when 2019 ended and I hadn't published any books. I had to analyze the situation to try to discover why this was. After careful study I discovered the reason – I DIDN'T WRITE ENOUGH! Now, that really surprised me!

To rectify the situation, I resolved that for 2020 I would write every day. And I have, every day this year. Almost 20,000 words – year-to-date. I'm working on three books. (1) *My Name Is Frank – The Biography, Genealogy, and Sermons of the Rev. Francis D. Daley*, (2) *ebay Sales – How to Sell Stuff on ebay*, and (3) *Revolt on Ganymede – an Alizar Adventure.*

My Name Is Frank is almost finished. It needs to be edited and proofread. To paraphrase Phil Fleck, it's time to shoot the author and print. *ebay Sales* needs some work on not making mistakes (more on that later). *Revolt on Ganymede* is in plot trouble. I've got a great beginning, a snappy and surprise ending but the in-between is eluding me.

Writing Report [5]

This is a follow-up to my email last March when I revealed that my writing hadn't been going as well as expected:-- ***Desired/Wished/Hoped.*** I resolved at the beginning of 2020 to write every day to see if that would produce more book publication.

As you would expect – that worked. As of January 1, 2021, I had written every day for 368 days. Total production was 96,480 words.

And I finished 5 books:

I.   "My Name is Franks" – My Father's Biography and a collection of his sermons.

II.   "A Friend of Bill's" – My Father's Biography

III.   "Alcoholism" – A collection of my Father's sermons on alcoholism

IV.   "Have you ever Been Afraid" – My Father's Sermon's

V.   "The Tooth of Time" – A collection of my poems

---

[5] Emailed on January 5, 2021 to a list of friends and foes - Daley News #42

So, I'm going to try to keep that going in 2021. I've got several books that are starting to shape up. Maybe I'll be inspired to tackle the Sci-fi stories again: -- the Adventures of Alizar. **Stay tuned!**

ebay Screwup[6]

As you may know, I've been selling stuff on ebay. When we moved from Reading to Florida and cleaned out the Reading house, there was a lot of stuff that was too good to throw out but not good enough to keep. So, I've been selling it on ebay. Usually this has gone off without a hitch, but every once in a while…

On February 10th, this year I had two sales, a Boy Scout Scout-sign pin and a patch that said, "Ride it Like you Stole it" Two different orders and two different customers both from Texas. Big deal in my ebay store. I packed the orders and shipped them.

On February 16th I got a message – "I received the wrong item. What I was sent was a pin with 3 fingers sticking up and not a Black & Orange patch "Ride It Like You Stole It."

Messaged him back, "Please send it back to me, I'll pay postage." Sent the same message to the pin customer. The pin was returned in a few days, with $25.30 postage due. Got a message from the patch customer. He had tried to send the patch back – "Return to Sender." The Post Office wasn't having any part of that. He said he'd send it again. I sent each customer a copy of one of my books and again expressed how sorry I was. Sent the pin to the pin

---

[6] Emailed to friends and family on March 31, 2020 – Daley News #4

customer. Was afraid I wasn't going to get the patch back, so I ordered another patch from Thailand. Got the original patch in the mail. Sent the patch to the patch customer. I sent messages to both customers asking how much postage I owed them   Both said I didn't owe them anything. Patch customer left feedback – "Great product & fast shipping!"

Anybody want a patch that reads – "Ride it Like you Stole it." See my ebay store. Do I lead an exciting life or what?

Will you make me a sandwich? [7]

Darnall's Rule #5 – "Many a man has been convicted of a crime that existed only in his wife's mind." (*Rules for Life*, p. 19) As you know, my bride and I are working on our 63rd year, so you may assume that I'm an authority on this subject. And there's no statute of limitations on these crimes. Furthermore, constitutionally *ex post facto* laws are prohibited but maritally they would appear to be allowed.

So, the other evening I asked her if she would make me a sandwich. "No". And why is that I asked. "Because you told me I don't know how to make sandwiches."

Not remembering that conversation and since it was not my first day at the rodeo, I asked the next question, "When was that?"

"Oh, shortly after we got married."

You see! No statute of limitation. Life is grand if you don't weaken.

Uncle Rob's Picture [8]

The story goes that my Uncle Rob (Robert Trimble 1864-1931, my Grandmother's oldest brother) lived in New York in the 1880's. He said that all his friends had these big oil paintings of their ancestors hung on the wall. So, to be part  of the in crowd, he bought a reproduction of a painting. He had it mounted in big, gilded frame and hung it on his wall. He told everyone, tongue in cheek I'm sure, that it was a painting of his ancestor.

 The painting shows a young woman playing a viola da gamba. For many years that painting hung on our wall in Wyomissing. For those years I had wondered who the artist was. I took pictures of the painting and showed it to folks at the Reading Museum. No one could identify it.

---

[8] Emailed to friends and family on April 21 - 2020 Daley News #7
This is the essay that gives this book its title.

Then one day Ernie and I were watching "Gunsmoke." (It was episode 31, season 8," Panacea Sykes." The show originally aired April 13, 1963.) Panacea, an elderly lady, is waiting to board the stage for Dodge. She doesn't have the fare, but says Kitty is her daughter. The driver, Alvy, says she's good for it. In Dodge Alvy gets the $1.75 from Kitty. Pan tells Kitty many a time you said I was like a mother to you. Kitty's dad was a gambler. When Kitty's mom died Pan took her in. So, Kitty

sets her up in a room upstairs in the Long Branch Saloon. When the scene switches to the room, there's Uncle Rob's picture! On the wall! In a room in the Long Branch Saloon!

Now that's too good a story for me not to retell. And when I told the story to a friend, he reminded me that I could scan the picture with my cell phone and Google would identify it for me. So, I did, and it did. I scanned the painting, and Google came back immediately with – Sir Anthony Van Dyke – "Portrait of Mary Ruthven, wife of the artist." *So now we know!*

We Wrote Letters [9]

Back in the day we wrote letters. There was no Facebook or Instagram. There was no internet nor email. At the military boarding school where Mother sent me as a reward for my good behavior, the only telephones we had access to were pay phones. Pay phones cost a nickel. You had to wait in line until the phone was available. If you called the girl's school, you had to hope the girl you were calling was near the phone. Phones were no joy.

So, we wrote letters. Stamps were three cents. (That's $0.32 in 2020 dollars.) We wrote to our parents. We wrote to our brothers and sisters. We wrote to our girlfriends. And they wrote back. If you wanted to get letters, you had to write letters. There was a post office station in the basement of one of the school buildings. It was enclosed in a wire cage next to the school store. One of the storekeepers was the designated postmaster. Our mail was sent care of General Delivery

McDonogh School
McDonogh, Maryland.

To get our mail we would line up just outside the post office and if we had a letter (or even better, a package!) the postmaster would give it to you. The

---

[9] Emailed to friends and family on April 28, 2020 – Daley News #8

first letter I ever got from my sweet bride was sent to me at school. It was addressed to "Donald Darnell." The postmaster said, "Here, Daley, this one's got to be yours." **The rest as they say is history.**

Grace [10]

When my father was in college and seminary, it was the custom for the students to go out on Sunday and conduct an afternoon service and an evening service at nearby mission churches. Between services one of the parishioners would invite the starving young students back to their house for a Sunday dinner. At one such meal the man of the house asked my father to say Grace. Trying to be polite my father said, "No, you go ahead." This turned into an embarrassing situation when it was revealed that the man did not know how to say Grace. My father said that for the rest of his life whenever someone asked him to say Grace the next words out of his mouth where always, "Let us pray…"

Six years of meals at McDonogh School prepared me to deal with that situation. In the dining hall before each meal we stood more or less quiet behind our chairs. The officer of the day resplendent in full military regalia including a red sash and saber would step up, tuck his cap under his left arm and command, "Let us Pray."

For the blessings we are about to receive,
O Lord, make us truly thankful. This we ask
in Christ's Name. Amen.

---

[10] Emailed to friends and family on May 5, 2020 – Daley News #9

I, nowadays, almost always resist the
temptation to give the next command,
"Cadets, Attention, Seats." **Almost always!**

Coach George "Pee Wee" Harris [11]

We had some wonderful teachers at McDonogh School, the military boarding school where Mother sent me as a reward for my good behavior. One of these was Coach George "Pee Wee" Harris. Coach Harris was a big-hearted mountain of a man who was a lot smarter than he played. In 1953 he was the shop teacher, and he was the line coach for the varsity football team. The head coach was Howard "Dutch" Eyth.

We were outside at mid-week football practice and working on offensive line blocking assignments. "Pee Wee" says, "75, you missed that block." He usually didn't bother to remember our names, but he had our numbers. Bob Bailey was number 75.

"But, Coach, inertia was against me." Bailey was just showing off. Some of us liked to pretend that we paid attention in our science classes.

In a flash "Pee Wee" called for help. "Hey, 'Dutch,' What's inertia?" Coach Eyth was way across the field and too far away to help. So, we kept going until Bailey overcame inertia.

----

[11] Emailed to friends and family on May 12, 2020 – Daley News #10

Coach George "Pee Wee" Harris [12]

Coach "Pee Wee" Harris was also the shop teacher. We learned woodwork, metal work and printing. We learned printing using a printing press that, many believed, had originally belonged to Ben Franklin.

In addition to being our coach, and the shop teacher, "Pee Wee" would referee high school football games that didn't involve McDonogh. If one of the players complained to him about one of his calls, he had these little calling cards that he had printed in his print shop. The cards in "Old English" script read:

> Your story has touched my heart. Never before have I met anyone with so many troubles as you have. Please accept this card as a token of my sincere sympathy.

Undoubtedly these little cards saved him untold hours of useless conversation.

Bart Harrison [13]

When I arrived at McDonogh in 1950 I was ill prepared academically, nor had I developed the discipline necessary to succeed academically. But not to worry. McDonogh School was starting their 77th year and they had a plan.

Our 7th grade English teacher was Mr. Bart Harrison. Bart was an iconoclast and exactly the right type for these boys being rewarded for their good behavior.

Bob "Put" Parks remembers him as the teacher that threw him out the window of his classroom. "Put" had the top bunk and I had the bottom bunk in our Lyle Building 3rd floor dormitory.

At one-point Bart learned that his classroom on the 1st floor of the Finney Building was going to be repainted. So, Bart tells us, "You guys always wanted to write on the walls, so go to it." We then proceeded to write on the walls of the classroom. It turned out that it took multiple coats of paint to cover the scribbles.

---

[13] Emailed to friends and family on May 26, 2020 – Daley News #12

A fact I'm sure Mr. Harrison got to discuss with somebody. [14]

During the 1st week of school, the English assignment was to pen a hundred-word essay. I either didn't turn it in or what I turned in wasn't satisfactory. In any case when the weekly academic deficiencies were posted, there was my name for English. Included with this posting was an invitation to come to school on Saturday for a three-hour study hall assignment. Unbeknownst to me when you failed a subject for the **week**, you got these extra study hall sessions. And attendance was not optional. (I wonder, do they still do this?)

Now I wasn't stupid at this point (I got that way only recently) I was merely ill informed. I only had to go to that Saturday session once. Once was enough for me to get the message. In view of the hundreds of essays I've written and published since then, I'm sure Bart Harrison would be amazed at my progress. **Thanks, Mr. Harrison, wherever you are.**

---

[14] Private interview with Chris Harrison (Bart Harrison's son) by email 5/26/2020. " …he did get to discuss the whole painting incident with the powers. Something about conduct unbecoming to the uniform. No credit was awarded for stimulating students, impromptu teamwork, or coloring inside the lines. Alas!"

Wonderful Lessons [15]

The schoolwork at McDonogh School was at times exciting for me. I remember learning that tintinnabulation and splash were examples of onomatopoeia. Learning that Darnall Daley was alliterative was illuminating.

However, I recently learned a rule of grammar that I had never been taught. If English is your native language, then you also know this rule, but you were never taught it either.

We say "flip-flop" and "ding-dong" but we would never say, "flop-flip" or "dong-ding." We might say, "Ding, dang, dong." We would never say "dong, dang, ding." Why is that?

The rule is that if there are three words then the order must be I, A, and O. If there are two words, then the first is I and then the second is either A or O. This is called **ablaut reduplication**. The rule seems inviolable. All four of the horse's feet make the same sound but we always, always say clip-clop never clop-clip.

Tock-tick children, time is up. That's our lesson for today.

---

[15] Emailed to friends and family on June 2, 2020 – Daley News #13

Latin [16]

In the 9th grade at McDonogh School we were allowed to take Latin. You know:

Latin is a dead language
As dead as dead can be
First it killed the Romans
And now it's killing me.

In spite of this popular opinion about Latin, I rather enjoyed it. I can still remember the 1st line in the 1st year textbook. *Discipupi picturae spectate.* (Students look at the picture.) Mr. Green was the Latin teacher and a really nice old guy. He retired after the 1952-1953 school year. I remember that a bunch of us went to visit him after he retired.

The second-year Latin book was <u>Caesars's Gallic Wars.</u> *Gallia est omnis divisa in partes tres…*(All Gaul is divided into three parts…) Mr. Green's replacement was ill suited to teach boys being rewarded for their good behavior. I'm afraid we treated him rather badly, especially after we caught

---

[16] Emailed to friends and family on June 9, 2020 – Daley News #14

him sneaking a girl into his rooms in Lyle building. As I recall, he didn't last the full year. The study of <u>Caesars's Gallic Wars</u> was made a lot easier when we discovered that you could buy a "pony." That's an interlinear translation.

My next brush with Latin was in my senior year. All the seniors lived in the Jane Bay Building [17] and our accommodations were palatial. We had a bed, a closet, and a little desk where we could do our homework. With great effort I fashioned a poster with fancy lettering for the wall over my desk – *Habe coitum quod ad sexum pertinent, id est magnus.* (Sex is great! Not that I actually knew but I had heard rumors.) Even though our senior room inspection was perfunctory, it was done every day by a teacher. One morning inspection was by a teacher who could read Latin. "Very funny, Daley. Take it down." He then proved that it was unusual but not impossible for a Cadet Major to get demerits. Well, what would you expect from boys being rewarded for their **good** behavior?

---

[17] This building has since been demolished.

Badminton [18]

When I was at Johns Hopkins, freshmen were required to take two semesters of a course – Physical Education. Because I was on the football team, I was excused from the first semester. But come the second semester I had to take the course. I remember that I was greatly put out by this. I thought I should have been excused from both semesters and that the course was a waste of my valuable time.

The first class was about badminton. I was busy making an ass out of my self and complaining loudly that badminton was such a sissy sport and why should I have to learn about that, *etc.*

About that time Professor Kelso Morrill happened to walk through the gym. Dr. Morrill taught the beginning math courses – analytic geometry and differential calculus to freshmen. I was well known to Dr. Morrill because of my struggles with analytic geometry. Of course, Dr. Kelso Morrill was better known for lacrosse. He played for the Hopkins 1925-1927 teams; he was on the 1928 US Olympic lacrosse team and was the national champion Hopkins coach from 1935 to 1950.

---

[18] Emailed to family and friends on September 29, 2020 – Daley News #29

Professor Morrill listened to my tirade for a few seconds and then said, "Don't go anywhere. Daley. I'll be right back." He returned a few minutes later in proper gym attire, "Ok, Daley, let's play some badminton."

He then proceeded to give me a badminton lesson. I'm certain I never scored a point. He ran me side to side, front to back and back to front until I was stepping on my tongue.

"So, what do you think, Daley? Still think badminton is a sissy sport?" Think? I was having trouble breathing.

Belphegor's Prime [19]

In demonology, Belphegor is a demon, and one of the seven princes of Hell, who helps people make discoveries. He seduces people by suggesting to them ingenious inventions that will make them rich. Belphegor is the chief demon of the deadly sin known as Sloth in the Christian tradition.

A palindrome is a number, word, or a phrase that is the same forward or backward. For example, madam, or racecar. A palindromic number example is 121 or 1991.

A prime number is a positive integer greater than or equal to 1 that is not a product of two smaller natural numbers.

So, there we have three interesting facts. You may well wonder how ~~the Hell~~ in the world I'm going to tie them together. And the answer is:

Belphegor's palindromic prime:

1,000,000,000,000,066,600,000,000,000,001

That's (10^{30} + 666 x 10^{14} +1). It was discovered by Harvey Dubner. It contains the number of the beast, 666 (Rev. 13:15-18), bracketed by 13 zeros. The

---

[19] Emailed to friends and family on June 16, 2020 – Daley News #15.

total length of the number is 31 digits (13 backwards).

And you thought you wouldn't learn anything new and useful today. If you can't win a barroom bet with this, you're just not doing it right.

Dad's Master's Degree [20]

My father graduated from the University of the South in Sewanee, Tennessee with a Bachelor of Arts degree in 1925. In 1930 he got a Bachelor of Divinity degree.

In 1968 at 65 years old he decided to retire to a retirement community in Florida. As they were closing the deal, he discovered that the community had a minimum age, and his 2nd wife was too young.   So, the retirement plans had to be postponed until 1972.

In late 1971 he got a letter from the University of the South telling him that they were reviewing the work he did to get his Divinity degree and they had decided that he really should have gotten a master's degree. Forty-one years after he graduated in 1930! Seriously, 41 years later! In the letter was a little certificate that they said he could

---

[20] Emailed to some friends and family on October 20, 2020 – Daley News #31

pin to the edge of his bachelor's degree certificate or for $25.00, if he would return the original certificate, they would send him a new certificate.

At this point in his life, his search for serenity had led my father to the conclusion that the world was a pretty funny place. He had discovered that life had to be faced with a sense of humor. Getting this just a few months before his second retirement I'm sure Dad thought was pretty funny.

Right-Hand Rule [21]

The transistor was invented while I was in high school and was just becoming commercially available while I was in college. My college courses, however, were mostly about vacuum tube electronic circuits.

My first job out of college was with Westinghouse in the Defense Electronics Division. I was in a group designing and building a digital search radar system for the Navy (SGP-59). Since this was a transistor system much of what I had learned in college had to be unlearned and new stuff had to be learned.

My first assignment was to design a circuit. Since this was 60 years ago, I long ago forgot what the circuit was supposed to do. The design process was to design the circuit, breadboard the design and test it. After the design was proven, it had to be put on a printed circuit board about the size of a sheet of paper with the circuit repeated 8 times. The

---

[21] Emailed to friends and family on July 28, 2020 – Daley News #20

design process for the PC board was to layout the circuit with black tape on a mylar sheet. Once that was done, the mylar sheet was photographed and a printed circuit board was made from that. Each circuit, as I recall, had 4 transistors. These transistors were packaged in a metal can (designated TO5) a little smaller than a dime with three leads coming out of the bottom – one transistor per package.

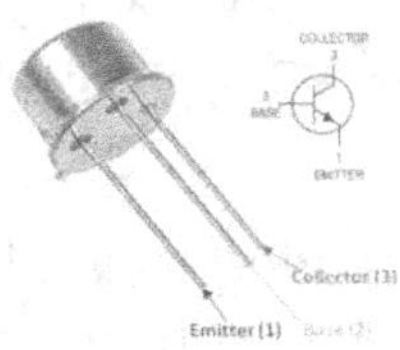

The mnemonic for the lead configuration was a right-hand rule using the thumb and two fingers of the right hand to represent these leads. The thumb was the collector, the first finger was the base, and the big finger was the emitter – leading, of course, to crude gestures.

Since we were on a tight schedule, I ordered 20 pieces of the PC board made. When they arrived, my technician and I assembled one of the boards. We tested it and it didn't work. One of life's "Oh Shit" moments. It seems that I had used the left-hand rule for all of the transistors, reversing the emitter and collector – 32 times. So, I reworked the PC layout and ordered 20 more pieces. New circuit boards arrived, and everything worked just fine.

I put the original, now useless, PC boards in my bottom desk drawer. If you could find that desk,

they're probably still there today, sixty years later.
Nobody throws that kind of stuff away.

Life and Times of Horatio Hornblower [22]

From my teenage years, I was a fan of C.S. Forester's Hornblower stories. It was a sadness for me when Forester's death in 1966 brought an end to these stores.

So, it was a delight when in 1970 the British naval historian, C. Northcote Parkinson, (Parkinson is better known for his management book, *Parkinson's Law*) published a biography of Horatio Hornblower, *Life and Times of Horatio Hornblower*, in which he revealed that Forester had based his famous stores on a real-life naval hero, Sir Horatio Hornblower. Parkinson did a wonderful job with this biography. There were pictures of Hornblower in uniform. A picture of Lady Hornblower and of the Hornblower estate. Not only did I read this book, but I talked about it with anybody who would listen including my Scouts (I was Scoutmaster of Troop 423) and their parents. I was enthralled.

A few months after the publication I was in the Baltimore County library and I found this book in the fiction section of the library. Now as a former student librarian I knew biographies should be in

---

the biography section filed alphabetically by subject. I pulled the book from the shelf and took it to the librarian to inquire about it being on the wrong shelf. She tells me, "Oh, I'm sorry, didn't you know? Parkinson's book is a totally fictional biography." She then pulls out a copy of a magazine (*The Librarian's Secret News* or some such) and shows me an article where the whole thing is explained (exposed!).

OOPS!

So now I had to go around and un-tell all the stores I had been telling. One of the people I had to let in on the secret was the father of one of my Scouts - he a history teacher at the Boys' Latin School[23] in Baltimore. He had been telling Hornblower stories to his students as historical fact. **And there you have it, fake news 50 years before we had fake news.**

---

[23] Actually, The Boys' Latin School of Maryland founded in 1844.

Too Much Fun [24]

The English teachers at McDonogh School gave us an appreciation for poetry. We were required to read poetry, write poetry, and to memorize poetry. Poetry comes to us today sometimes in the lyrics of the songs we hear. For example:

Blue lights flashing in my rear view
The sheriff said, "Boy I should've known it was you
You got fourteen people in the back of this truck
I warned you twice and now I'm writing you up"
I said "Officer, what have I done?"
He smiled and said, "Boy you're having too much fun"

Too much fun, what's that mean?
It's like too much money, there's no such thing
It's like a girl too pretty with too much class
Being too lucky, a car too fast
No matter what they say I've done
But I ain't never had too much fun

Sung by Daryle Singletary, this song was popular in 1995 when I was bringing my then six-year-old grandson (he's now 31) home from his first Cub Scout camp. I asked, "Did you have fun?"

---

[24] Emailed to friends and family on September 22, 2020 – Daley News #28. Some had fun with this story. Others exhibited no sense of humor.

"Oh, Pops, I had too much fun!" **Life recapitulates poetry!**

How Much does a Cloud Weigh [25]

Little cloud up in the sky,
I just watch you floating by.
Fluffy stuff doesn't seem like much,
Just bits of moisture and other such.
If I could find a place to stand,
Could I lift you? Now, that'd be grand.[26]

So how much does a cloud weigh? Well, let's do a little math. The moisture density in that fluffy cumulus you see on a bright day is about 0.5 grams per cubic meter. Let's say we see a cloud that's 1 kilometer wide by 2 kilometers long by 0.5 kilometer high. That's 1,000,000,000 cubic meters. With moisture at 0.5 grams per cubic meter we have 500,000 kilograms or 1,102,311 pounds.

Wow! Now to lift that sucker you'd need a really solid fulcrum and a really, really long lever.

---

[25] Emailed out to a group of friends and family on November 3, 2020.- Daley News #33. Some did the math and confirmed my conclusions.

[26] F. Darnall Daley, Jr., "Little Cloud," *The Tooth of Time*, 2020, p. 65

Camping at Catoctin Mountain National Park [27]

I read the other day that the President was going to spend the weekend at Camp David. Camp David is the presidential retreat located in the Catoctin Mountain National Park. There's a youth camping area in the Catoctin Mountain Park that's right next to Camp David. 45 years ago, this spot was a regular stop on the camping itinerary of Boy Scout Troop 423 (Darnall Daley – Scoutmaster).

On one of our trips to Catoctin Mountain my son, running through the woods, fell and split his arm open near the elbow. The cut was about 2 inches long and when his arm was bent at the elbow was 2 inches wide.

Leaving the other leaders with the troop I took my son in search of medical assistance. For some reason unbeknownst to me now, a couple or three other Scouts came along. The Park Rangers directed us to a country doctor's office a few miles away from the park.

Without much delay the doctor started to apply stiches to the cut. The informality of the setting

---

[27] Emailed to Family and friends on July 14, 2020 – Daley News #19

allowed the non-wounded Scouts to gather around to observe and supervise the operation.

Seeing that he had an audience the doctor said, "You Scouts should recognize the knot I'm using, it's called a square knot."

To my chagrin, I then heard one of my Scouts say. "Actually, Doctor, most doctors use a surgeon's knot, but we call the knot that you just tied a granny knot." **Life's little moments!**

Mormon or Viking Afterlife [28]

It is my understanding that members of the Church of Jesus Christ of the Latter-Day Saints (LDS) or the Mormons believe that families are eternal, if "sealed" through an appropriate temple ceremony. Not only can living members of the family be "sealed" in this manner but ancestors that died without these ceremonies can also be thus united with their families. Hence, the LDS interest in genealogy.

Now I don't know what the Mormon afterlife might be like but surely it can't be as much fun as that believed in by our Viking warrior ancestors.

The afterlife for all Viking warriors, that Odin deemed worthy, was to go to Valhalla. There they would fight all day. At night, restored to full health from any of their battle wounds, they would feast, and drink mead all night waited on by beautiful maidens called Valkyrie.

---

[28] Emailed to family and friends on June 30, 2020 – Daley News #17

Which leads me to an irreverent thought. A present-day Mormon descendant of a 9th century Viking warrior has an appropriate temple ceremony performed. Can't you just imagine the bewilderment of one of our Norse ancestors suddenly yanked from Valhalla into the Mormon afterlife. I'll bet that's an interesting family reunion.

Yogi Berra [29]

I just saw this on Facebook.

"Just because something is on Facebook doesn't necessarily mean it's true." – William Shakespeare

Attributing a saying or a quote to an individual is tricky. If I quote:

"Everything on the internet is true." – Abraham Lincoln

That's obviously suspect. But if I say:

"Everything on the internet is true." – Jimmy Kimmel

Now that's more reasonable. He could have said that. You don't know. You can't prove he never said that. You might think he might have said that by finding it in print from something he wrote or something that was written about him.

---

[29] Sent by email to friends and foe alike on December 8, 2020. Some were delighted to receive it, others not so much – Daley News #38

You might find a video of him saying this. However, with the computer programs that are available today to manipulate video, I'm not sure what that would prove.

A poem I always liked, and I thought, was by Ogden Nash.

> What a strange beast is the flea,
> You can't tell he from she
> But he can
> And so, can she.

But apparently it was not written by Ogden Nash. So, the point is that attributing quotes is really tricky.

One of the most quoted people of all time has to be Yogi Berra, the famous New York Yankee catcher. He had a unique way of thinking and speaking. For example:

"It ain't over 'til it's over!"

"Nobody goes there anymore. It's too crowded."

"It's *déjà vu* all over again."

"I usually take a two-hour nap, from 1 to 4."

And my favorite:

"When you come to a fork in the road, take it."

As often as he was quoted, he was also often misquoted. So much so that Yogi felt compelled to write a book - ***The Yogi Book : I Really Didn't Say Everything I Said*** [30]

---

[30] Berri, Yogi, *The Yogi Book: I Really Didn't Say Everything I Said,* Workman Publishing Company, New York, 1999

Game Day Breakfast [31]

We marched to all our meals at McDonogh School. As I remember, we were well fed. There was always milk to drink. All you could want. Every table had a pitcher. When it was empty, the biddy (Cadet waiter) would take it to the kitchen and fill it from a big, refrigerated tank. There was always plenty to eat.

Of course, sometimes there was monotony and predictability to the menus. For example, Sunday night supper was melted cheese on toast, canned pear halves, and vanilla cookies for dessert. Every Sunday night! For years!

But the best meal of all was the game-day breakfast for the football team. On the Friday morning before a football game the football team all ate together. Our breakfast was a dinner-plate sized T-bone steak, baked potato, and ice cream for dessert. **Now that's a breakfast.**

---

[31] Emailed to family and friends on July 7, 2020 – Daley News #18

A Republic if You Can Keep It [32]

We have had three governments of the United States of America. The first was a revolutionary cabal known as the Continental Congress. The second was under the Articles of Confederation. This constitution was ratified on March 1, 1781 when the Articles were signed by John Hanson, the delegate to the Continental Congress from Maryland and my 5-great-granduncle. The Articles of Confederation were flawed in several respects (but that's an article for another day).

So, in the hot summer of 1787 the greats and near greats of the American political scene gathered in Philadelphia to craft a new government and a new constitution. They decided at the beginning of their gathering to work in secret. They even closed the windows in this age long before air conditioning or deodorant to prevent leaks. And apparently, they were able to do their work in secret. No leaks about what they were doing the whole summer.

When their work was concluded and they were ready to publish their new constitution, Ben Franklin was asked by a prominent Philadelphia socialite and wife of the Philadelphia Mayor, Mrs. Elizabeth Willing Powel, "What do we have a republic or a monarchy?"

---

[32] Sent out lovingly to a number of friends and family on November 10, 2020.- Daley News #34

Franklin famously answered, "A republic, Madam, if you can keep it." **The jury is still out about that, isn't it?**

USS Bonhomme Richard [33]

The fire aboard the USS Bonhomme Richard in the San Diego Naval Base recently got me to thinking about another USS Bonhomme Richard, a 42-gun ship in the revolutionary war US Navy. [34]

The Captain of this revolutionary war ship was John Paul Jones sometimes called the "Father of the American Navy" and later a rear admiral in the Imperial Russian Navy.

It was at the Battle of Flamborough Head that Captain John Paul Jones was famously, but perhaps apocryphally, quoted saying, "I have not yet begun to fight," when it was demanded that he surrender his ship.

It was at this point that another famous saying was born. A wounded sailor was lying in the scuppers of the embattled ship. He was bloody, beaten about

---

[33] Because I'm such a generous guy, this story was shared with friends by email on December 1, 2020. What a guy! It was Daley News #37

[34] It's just been announced that because the damage from the fire is so extensive that the ship will have to be scrapped.

the head and body. When he heard his captain say,
"I have not yet begun to fight," he was heard to say,
"Yeah, there is always that 10% that don't get the
word." And the rest as THEY say is history.

How I Met Your Grandmother [35]

There's a TV show – "How I Met Your Mother." I could write about how I met your mother but the audience for that is limited. Instead I'll write about how I met your grandmother. Much broader interest. *I often tell this story, so you may have heard it before.*

In the middle of the last century my mother apparently reached the end of her patience. I never was told what the defining act was, but she reached the end of her rope. She arranged for me to be entered into a military school – McDonogh School. This, of course, changed my life. There were many things that were different, but one was we had dancing class. At dancing class, we learned the waltz, the foxtrot, and the Mexican Hat dance. Picture, if you will all, these 7th grade boys all dressed in their full-dress military uniforms. From what I've told you so far that image would be incomplete. No girls. McDonogh was an all-boy's school in those days.

---

[35] Emailed to family and friends on September 8, 2020 – This was Daley News #26

So, they trucked girls in from some of the surrounding girl's schools. One of the schools so honored was Samuel Ready School. And one of those little girls, then 11 years old, was my bride Ernie Geist.

Of course, my story is that she fell in love with me on first sight. Her story is a little different. She did fall for one of those cute cadets, but it wasn't me. It was my classmate, Kim Webb. This was a surprise to Kim's wife when I told this story at dinner one night many years later at Kim's house in Massachusetts.

Robert White [36]

We had some wonderful teachers at McDonogh School. One of those was Robert "Bob" White. Bob White taught plane geometry. The Bobwhite is also a North American ground dwelling bird also known as the Virginia Quail that has a very distinctive call – tweet-TWEET. Just because he was a wonderful teacher doesn't mean we treated him properly and with respectful decorum. Bear in mind that this was a room full of boys being rewarded for their good behavior! He would turn his back to the class to write on the blackboard and a bird from the

bobwhite flock would tweet-TWEET from the back of the classroom.

He would turn to see who had tweet-TWEETED, but he could never catch them. Looking back, I don't have the sense that the bird chorus bothered him all that much. I can imagine him chuckling and telling the other teachers that he had a flock of birds in his class today.

---

[36] Emailed to family and friends on August 25, 2020 – Daley News #24

In truth I loved plane geometry. Bob White made it crystal clear. Bob White loved plane geometry. He passed that love on to some of us. Even today, 67 years later, I can still prove some of those plane geometry theorems.

tweet-TWEET!

No Seat Belts [37]

When I was at McDonogh School there were three brothers, the Boccuti brothers, Anthony was older, Salvatore in my class (the class of 1956) and Oscanio (aka "Sconni") who was a year younger.

On one occasion, Sconni asked me to get him a date. I got him a date with Sylvia Landis, a really cute gal who had been in my class at Roland Park Public School. It seems that my bride was not my date that night. (I asked her! She remembers me telling this story but claims she wasn't there.)

Now believe it or not there was a day when our cars didn't have seat belts. (They didn't become mandatory in American cars until January 1, 1968.) We picked up Sylvia at her house on the York Road. Sconni was driving. We hadn't gone two blocks when he had to jam on the brakes because a car stopped suddenly in front of us. Sylvia slid off the seat, down onto the floor, and under the dashboard.

There she was curled up on the floor, perhaps injured. Oscanio Boccuti looks over at her and in a very serious voice commands, "Sit still, honey!" Needless to say, that was not the beginning of a budding romance.

---

[37] Emailed to family and friends on August 18, 2020 Daley News #23

Rear Admiral William E. Verge [38]

At McDonogh School, if you did something wrong, you were put on a report. Every day the "Delinquency Report" was posted at several prominent places around the school. The report listed your name, the offense, the potential number of demerits, and who "put you on" report. The "who" was either a faculty member or a cadet officer. Demerits had to be worked off at certain acceptable tasks at the rate of 45 minutes per demerit. There was a menu of what each piece of dumbness was worth. For example, late for class was a two-demerit offense.

The next step in the process was for you to answer the delinquency. You had two choices for this. The first choice was to go to Robert "Iron Jaw" Lynch. [39] Mr. Lynch commanded the study hall. Reporting to him to answer delinquency was an experience. He had a voice that could break glass at 1000 yards.

---

[38] Emailed to family and friends on August 11, 2020 - Daley News #22

[39] Email interview with Mary Jean Lynch Spencer – "What you all didn't know was that the 'Jaw' was all iron on the outside and marshmallow on the inside. Scared me sometimes but he was fair. I got the same kind of discipline as you all did!!" Mary Jean was Mr. Lynch's daughter.

He was not shy about telling you what an idiot you were. However, if you needed a quiet word of encouragement, he would give that to you in a much quieter voice. He also liked a good story and, if you came up with a story he liked, he might let you off.

REAR ADMIRAL WILLIAM E. VERGE

Your other choice was to go to the commandant. In my first years this was Rear Admiral William E. Verge. Admiral Verge was a 1924 Naval Academy graduate and WWII veteran. He came to McDonogh in 1947. He was, as I remember, a pretty stern customer. You would walk into his office, salute, and announce that you were there to answer the delinquency report. If you were smart, you had a story ready. But right in your line of vision on his desk was a little plaque – "Please remember, there is a difference between good sounding reasons and good sound reasoning."

So, when asked, "OK, Daley, what's your story?" you might just say, "No excuse, sir!" I'm sure that little plaque saved him thousands of hours of useless conversation.

Of course, sometimes you weren't given a reporting choice. For example, a breakfast announcement, "Cadet Daley will report to the Commandant's Office immediately after breakfast." Fun times!

McDonogh Morning Schedule [40]

The morning schedule at McDonogh School, as I remember, went something like this.

6:45 AM – Reveille - This was quite a production. It was presided over by the Officer of the Day in full regalia including a red sash and saber drawn to salute the flag. There was a bugler to sound the reveille bugle call. There were two or three cadets to raise the American flag and then there was the cadet who fired off the cannon at exactly 6:45 to start the whole parade.

7:00 AM – Breakfast formation. Off we would march to the dining hall.

7:30 to 8:30 AM – Morning work program. Everybody had a work assignment. These included things like cleaning the school buildings. You could be assigned to work at the horse barn or the cow barn. You could also arrange to be assigned to a different job if there was an opening. My assignment of choice in 8th and 9th grade was the green house. If your job got you dirty, you could be excused from inspection to take a shower to get

---

[40] Emailed to family and friends October 13, 2020 – Daley News #30

ready for class. In the 10th grade I got an assignment of operating the school PBX switchboard from 7:30 to 8:30 AM before the school opened. I wanted to keep that job in my senior year, but they made me supervise the cleaning one of the buildings.

8:45 AM – Inspection at your bunk dressed for classes.

9:00 AM – First class of the day.

But, of course, we were younger then!

"Strong In, Strong Out" by Dick Virgilio [41]

I just finished reading *"Strong In, Strong Out."* This is the autographical story of the life of Dick Virgilio. Dick was a classmate at McDonogh School. Another classmate, Jon Nevins, told me about this book and urged me to read it.

A 13-year-old runaway, a naval doctor in a Vietnam MASH, a skilled Navy trauma surgeon, the "Father of San Diego Trauma System," a world class sailing adventurer, the loving father of 5 children and grandfather of 9, and the devoted husband of a girl he loved at 1st sight when he was in medical school, Dick Virgilio's story is of a life well lived. Virgilio and co-author Joe Ditler have crafted a story that's a really good read. The hair-raising tale of his first long ocean sail from San Diego to Hawaii is well worth the read all by itself.

Get a copy and read it. You'll love it!

---

[41] Lovingly emailed to friends on January 12, 2021.- Daley News #43

Varsity Sunbathing [42]

At McDonogh School after class in the afternoon we had an athletic period. Everybody had to participate in something. In the fall I played football. During the winter period I think I played basketball. I don't remember for sure. None of the spring sports held any interest for me. I discovered that I could go down to the greenhouse and work there with Coach Ken Horner. Fortunately, this got gardening out of my system at an early age. I've had no interest in that since.

In the fall of my sophomore year I decided to go out for the varsity football team. Much to my very great surprise (and everybody else, too) I made the team. Because I had been on a varsity team, they told me that I had to go out for a varsity team during the winter and spring periods, too.

Since I knew Coach Ken Horner from my greenhouse days, I went out for varsity wrestling. The wrestling team had a room in the basement of the Field House. The coach sat crossed legged again the North wall and issued his instructions. For each weight class there was a hierarchy with the number one wrestler being the one that represented the school in the dual meets. Guys

---

[42] Emailed to friend and foe alike on November 17, 2020. – Daley News #35

would challenge to move up in this hierarchy. McDonogh was a wrestling powerhouse in those days with state champions in most weight classes. Names like Irv Naylor, Charlie Nichols, Bob Pac, and Jack Cooper come to mind. The only way I would ever get in a dual meet would have been if 10 or 12 guys got sick. But the wrestling room was warm, and it was a nice place to be in the winter.

When the spring came, as I noted, I had no interest in any of the spring sports. I decided that the least bad choice was track. So, I went out for the track team. The coach was Coach Stroh. On the first day he gathered everybody and questioned their intent. "Why are you here?" he'd ask. Guys would answer, "I want to run the mile." I want to run the high hurdles." "I want to do the high jump"

When it came my turn, "I'm here because they made me."

"Oh yes," said Coach Stroh, "we've heard that before. You go down to the end of the field and work on your tan." And so, I did. That, Ladies and Gentlemen, is how I made the varsity sunbathing team. I was on that team for three years. For some unknown reason I never got my letter.

After Word

I hope you enjoyed this book. I'm always glad to hear from my readers. My email address is fdarnall@gmail.com. I try to answer all my messages. If you'd like me to email you when the next book is ready, please let me know. If you like this book, I hope you'll tell your friends. Ask your friends to tell their friends. Seriously, spread the word! Word of mouth is the only advertising I can afford. Signed copies are available on ebay. These make great birthday and Christmas presents. You might also leave an Amazon review. One sentence will do the trick. You could also like the Facebook page, if I ever get around to setting one up.